WHO IS JESUS?

IO190552

THE PUZZLE AND THE PORTRAITS OF A DIVINE SAVIOR

ALLAN R. BEVERE

Topical Line Drives
Volume 35

Energion Publications
Gonzalez, Florida
2019

ISBN10: 1-63199-693-2
ISBN13: 978-1-63199-693-1

Energion Publications
P. O. Box 841
Gonzalez, FL 32560

pubs@energion.com
energion.com

Table of Contents

This little book is dedicated to my granddaughters
Aly, Emery, Quinn, and Spencer.
May you be faithful followers
of our divine human Savior
all of your days.

INTRODUCTION

'Tis a Puzzlement

In Matthew, Mark, and Luke there is a pivotal moment in these Gospels where Jesus asks his disciples the question, "Who do you say that I am?" (Matthew 16:13-20; Mark 8:27-30; Luke 9:18-20). It is a crucial question that the New Testament reminds us must be answered. To avoid answering the question is to give an answer.

It is perhaps the case that no question has been bandied about more than this one. This is not surprising since Jesus is one of the most influential historical figures in world history. It is also not surprising that not everyone is in agreement as how to answer this question, "Who is Jesus?"

I hope this little book will provide a helpful summary as I attempt to provide my own answer to that question—but it is not my answer that I have come up with on my own. As will become clear, I cannot think about the person of Jesus, the doctrine of Christology, without the wisdom of the church. I am not smart enough to think for myself on such deep matters; I need the wisdom of the ages to help me answer that same question Jesus posed to his first disciples two thousand years ago. I must answer it; for I am a disciple too. You must answer as well.

CHAPTER ONE

The Jesus Puzzle

PUTTING IT TOGETHER

I'm not a fan of jigsaw puzzles, especially the ones with 1000 pieces or more. I simply do not have the patience. But for those who enjoy such recreational activities, the one thing every puzzler knows is that the photo on the box top is necessary for completing the puzzle. It's the photo that offers the big picture for a thousand scattered pieces on the table.

I think this analogy helps us to answer the question, "Who is Jesus?" Our quest is like putting together the pieces of the puzzle given to us by the Old Testament that once completed will give us the portrait of Jesus we find in the New Testament. Think of the Old Testament as the pieces of the puzzle with the New Testament offering to us the picture on the top of the box. Now, this analogy is not perfect (no analogy ever is) because the New Testament portrayals of Jesus are somewhat like a puzzle as well, but the Old Testament in and of itself cannot complete the picture of Jesus. We need the New Testament to bring the picture into focus because it is Jesus who gives clarity to the Old Testament puzzle; and the best source for knowing Jesus is the New Testament.

But first, we must scatter the Old Testament pieces out on the table and begin to make sense of what is before us.

THE OLD TESTAMENT: PIECES IN RANDOM ORDER

Over the years, Christians have said to me, "I don't understand why so many Jews don't believe in Jesus. It is obvious from the Old Testament that Jesus is the Messiah." But is it? Does the Old Testament itself provide a clear picture of the coming deliverer that it is obviously Jesus? When Christians make such claims, we must remember that we do so looking at the Old Testament through the lens of the New. Christians believe that the Old Testament points to Jesus, but we cannot know that without Jesus himself. So, how do we understand the Old Testament in and of itself?

Let's return to the puzzle analogy. Suppose you had your one thousand pieces in front of you, but no box top with the picture of the completed puzzle. You could still work on the puzzle fitting pieces together, trying to match each piece according to the shape and colors of each piece. It would take much longer not knowing the completed picture but getting enough pieces together would begin to give you portions, let's call them glimpses, of what the puzzle is like. Now add to that this wrinkle: suppose that half of the pieces are missing. Even if you manage to get half the puzzle together without the box top, you would still have an incomplete picture. Without those five hundred missing pieces, you cannot know the full portrait you are attempting to assemble.

That's what we have with the Old Testament—it is the puzzle that ultimately points to Jesus as the Messiah, but some of the pieces are missing and that prevents us from getting the full picture. That makes the New Testament not only the box top that provides us with the completed picture, but it also provides us with the missing pieces. It would be like receiving five hundred pieces in a plastic bag and not being able to get the rest of the pieces and the picture of the puzzle until after the first half of the puzzle is put together. Moreover, we might fail to select some of those pieces leaving them off to the side (perhaps because don't think those pieces fit) which makes the picture even more incomplete. So, it is not obvious from the Old Testament itself that Jesus is the Messiah. We need the Old Testament to be sure, but more than that is necessary if we are to answer the question, "Who is Jesus?"

THE NEW TESTAMENT: RESURRECTION GLASSES—THE PICTURE COMES INTO FOCUS

As I write these words, I am wearing my bifocals. Without the lenses of my glasses that bring the words on this page into focus, it would be difficult to do what I am doing right now. Since I wear glasses all of the time, I see the world through those lenses. In fact, all of us see the world through the "lenses" of our experience. Our joys and pains, our friends and family, the places where we have lived, and many other experiences are "lenses" through which we see the world. I not only wear glasses; I'm also diabetic, which means that when I see food, I not only see something delicious, but I also see a dish that may or may not make my blood sugar spike to a higher level. I see my diet through my health concerns. There is nothing wrong with seeing life through the lenses of our experience. That is just the way it is.

The writers of the New Testament viewed the Old Testament through their experience of the resurrected Jesus. Once they encountered Jesus in his resurrected life, they knew their Old Testament Scriptures pointed to him. But how? The apostles struggled to see it during Jesus' earthly ministry. It was only after seeing the empty tomb and encountering a once again alive Jesus that the pieces of the Jesus puzzle in the Old Testament began to fall in place. The story of Paul's conversion in Acts 9 gives to us a good example. It's a long story, but worth quoting in full.

> Meanwhile Saul, still breathing threats and murder against the disciples of the Lord, went to the high priest and asked him for letters to the synagogues at Damascus, so that if he found any who belonged to the Way, men or women, he might bring them bound to Jerusalem. Now as he was going along and approaching Damascus, suddenly a light from heaven flashed around him. He fell to the ground and heard a voice saying to him, 'Saul, Saul, why do you persecute me?' He asked, 'Who are you, Lord?' The reply came, 'I am Jesus, whom you are persecuting. But get up and enter the city, and you will be told what you are to do.' The men who were travelling with him stood speechless because they heard the voice but saw no one. Saul got up from the ground, and though his eyes were open, he could see nothing; so they led him by the hand and brought him into Damascus. For three days he was without sight, and neither ate nor drank.

> Now there was a disciple in Damascus named Ananias. The Lord said to him in a vision, 'Ananias.' He answered, 'Here I am, Lord.' The Lord said to him, 'Get up and go

to the street called Straight, and at the house of Judas look for a man of Tarsus named Saul. At this moment he is praying, and he has seen in a vision a man named Ananias come in and lay his hands on him so that he might regain his sight.' But Ananias answered, 'Lord, I have heard from many about this man, how much evil he has done to your saints in Jerusalem; and here he has authority from the chief priests to bind all who invoke your name.' But the Lord said to him, 'Go, for he is an instrument whom I have chosen to bring my name before Gentiles and kings and before the people of Israel; I myself will show him how much he must suffer for the sake of my name.' So Ananias went and entered the house. He laid his hands on Saul and said, 'Brother Saul, the Lord Jesus, who appeared to you on your way here, has sent me so that you may regain your sight and be filled with the Holy Spirit.' And immediately something like scales fell from his eyes, and his sight was restored. Then he got up and was baptized, and after taking some food, he regained his strength.

For several days he was with the disciples in Damascus, and immediately he began to proclaim Jesus in the synagogues, saying, 'He is the Son of God.' All who heard him were amazed and said, 'Is not this the man who made havoc in Jerusalem among those who invoked this name? And has he not come here for the purpose of bringing them bound before the chief priests?' Saul became increasingly more powerful and confounded the Jews who lived in Damascus by proving that Jesus was the Messiah. (Acts 9:1-22)

We know from earlier in Acts that Saul (his name prior to becoming an apostle) vehemently opposed the first Christians and in Acts 9 he is on a mission to bring Christians in Damascus back to Jerusalem for trial. As a well-trained rabbi, he was certain that Jesus could not be the Messiah and he undoubtedly had his arguments from Scripture to support his views. But then on the Damascus

Road, he met the risen Jesus. Saul could no longer deny that Jesus was alive; and since God raises only the righteous, Jesus must be who his first followers claimed him to be.

That meant for Saul that he had been reading the Old Testament incorrectly. It did point to Jesus, but how? Now as the Apostle Paul, he needed to look at the Scriptures anew with resurrection glasses, and when we read his letters in the New Testament that is exactly what we discover. For Paul, Israel's Scriptures point to Jesus as the Messiah.

Indeed, when we read the books of the New Testament, all the writers are interpreting the Old Testament through resurrection lenses. The Gospel writers tell us that events in the life of Jesus fulfilled the Scriptures and the risen Jesus himself demonstrates to the two disciples on the road to Emmaus that the Old Testament points to him.

> Then he [Jesus] said to them, 'Oh, how foolish you are, and how slow of heart to believe all that the prophets have declared! Was it not necessary that the Messiah should suffer these things and then enter into his glory?' Then beginning with Moses and all the prophets, he interpreted to them the things about himself in all the scriptures. (Luke 24:25-27)

We will look more specifically at the portraits of Jesus painted by the four Gospels in chapter four, but for the moment two things must be said about the picture of the person of Jesus painted in the New Testament: Jesus is fully human and he is also fully divine. That is what the post New Testament generation of Christians concluded from looking back at the New Testament. If the first generation of believers needed the New Testament to make sense of the Old Testament, the next generation needed the New Testament to make sense of their doctrine concerning who Jesus was as Lord and Savior.

The Divine Human Puzzlement

Jesus is at the center of Christianity. It has been so since the beginning of the faith. But was Jesus human? Was Jesus divine? The New Testament seems to suggest two contradictory things.

On the one hand, the New Testament makes it clear that Jesus was a human being, made of flesh and bone with human needs and desires. Jesus did very human things we would never expect God to do: he ate (Luke 7:36), slept (Mark 4:38), bled, (John 19:34), and died (Matthew 27:50). Jesus also refers to God as his Father and calls himself God's Son, suggesting that he is someone different from God (John 17:1, 24). The Gospels give to us a very human Jesus.

One the other hand, there are statements in the Gospels that strongly suggest that Jesus was divine. Right at the beginning of John's Gospel we read, "In the beginning was the Word (that is, the Son), and the Word was with God, and the Word was God," (1:1) Jesus makes claims to divinity (John 14:9), though there are those who question whether such claims actually came from Jesus himself; and Jesus' favorite title for himself was "Son of Man (Matthew 11:19; 24:30; Mark 8:38; 9:31; Luke 6:5; 9:22; John 3:13; 13:31), which refers to a celestial figure in Daniel 7:13). In Luke's Gospel the disciples asked the same question many ask today.

> One day he got into a boat with his disciples, and he said to them, 'Let us go across to the other side of the lake.' So they put out, and while they were sailing he fell asleep. A gale swept down on the lake, and the boat was filling with water, and they were in danger. They went to him and woke him up, shouting, 'Master, Master, we are perishing!' And he woke up and rebuked the wind and the raging waves; they ceased, and there was a calm. He said to them, 'Where is your faith?' They were afraid and amazed, and said to one another, 'Who then is this, that he commands even the winds and the water, and they obey him?' (Luke 8:22-25)

"Who is this that he commands even the winds and the water, and they obey him?" Who alone can do such things other than God?

The post New Testament generation confronted in this a real dilemma. The Bible clearly states from Genesis to Revelation that there is only one God and the early Christians believed that whole-heartedly. Yet, there were statements in the Gospels and the rest of the New Testament that made implicit and explicit claims to the divinity of Jesus. This became even more confused with the portrayal of Jesus in the Gospels as a human being.

What was to be made of this? At first, it appears that the early church did not worry too much about how exactly to work out this dilemma. It seemed that the first believers were able to hold both of the ideas of Jesus' humanity and divinity together without thinking through much of the details. But as time went on, it became necessary to look at the issue more closely as the church was becoming bitterly divided over how to understand the person of Jesus particularly in relationship to God the Father. The only way to settle the question was to call a meeting of the entire church. So, in 325 A.D. a council was convened to fit together the Jesus puzzle.

CHAPTER TWO

The Puzzle Deconstructed: Failed Portraits and the Church's Response

BUSINESS TRIP: THE CHURCH'S FIRST GLOBAL GATHERING

By the first part of the third century A.D. it was clear that a solution to the Jesus puzzle was not going to be found without a meeting of the leaders of the church from all over the Roman Empire. So, the Emperor Constantine (born sometime after 280 A.D. and died in 337)[1] called for a church council that met in Nicaea (what is today İznik, Turkey). It was the first ecumenical or universal council because it was the first time church leaders from the eastern and western parts of the empire met together to come to a consensus on an issue.[2]

A BISHOP CREATES A CONTROVERSY

By the early second century, most Christians had come to believe that Christ was both divine and human. While these doctrines were held from the beginning, they were not always held easily. Then, as now, the assertion that a poor Jewish carpenter who died on a cross was God seemed absurd to many. Even though the Roman belief in the divinity of the emperor was embraced by loyal subjects in the ancient world, it was the Jewish background of Christianity contributed to this uneasiness about such a claim. The monotheism inherited from Judaism about divine claims in

---

1 Constantine the Great, who became the Roman Emperor of the western part of the empire in 312 A.D. and sole emperor in 324 A.D. until his death, did not care about the theological issues at stake. He was more concerned that the sharp disagreements in the church would divide the empire. So, he called the church council in an attempt to settle the argument only because he wanted to unify the people politically.

2 For a good overview of the Council of Nicaea, see Justo L. Gonzalez, *The Story of Christianity: The Early Church to the Dawn of the Reformation.* (San Francisco: Harper and Row, 1984), 1:158-167.

reference to Jesus sounded polytheistic. Some Jewish Christians (referred to as Ebionites) taught that Jesus was not divine at all. He was only human. He was a prophet. At best he was an angel.

While on the one side there was difficulty in accepting Christ's divinity, other groups of Christians referred to as Gnostics had conclude that Christ could not be human, since divinity was pure and could have no contact with the material world without being corrupted. Jesus only seemed to be human claimed the Docetists, whose name came from the Greek word *dokeō* which means "to seem" or "to appear."

The general consensus among Christians was to assert that Jesus was both human and divine. This position was not a compromise to the extremes. It was the only position the church could take and keep the integrity of the work of Christ in tact (more on that later). This position, which became known as the Orthodox view was not embraced by everyone. We must be careful not to be too harsh on those Christians who held a different perspective. They, like all theologians, were trying to understand the person of Jesus and his work of salvation. They were arguing for what they thought should be the orthodox position. The fact that the ecumenical church rejected their claims in no way suggests their sincerity in what they believed. A failed portrait should not cast moral doubt upon the painter.

As can be well imagined, when someone makes a statement like "the Son is both divine and human," someone will eventually ask that such a claim be explained. The first person who raised the question in a way that required a response was a priest in Alexandria named Arius.

Arius was not the first to have difficulty with the notion that Christ was both divine and human. What Arius did was put the question a little differently. The basic question had been, "How is Jesus Christ related to us?" Arius instead focused on "Who is Jesus Christ?' Is Jesus divine or is Jesus a creature?"[3]

---

3 The political motivations of the First Council of Nicaea are neither a concern of mine, nor significant for the theological consensus of the council. See Peter J. Leithart, *Defending Constantine: The Twilight of an Empire and the Dawn of Christendom*. (Downers Grove: InterVarsity Press, 2010), pp. 168-175.

It is important to say that as the church struggled over this second question, it was wise in that it knew whatever answer it would settle upon would greatly affect how it answered the first question. From early on the church placed questions about the person of Christ in the context of the work of Christ. "If we say thus and such about Jesus, what does it mean for our understanding of salvation?" Again, we must be reminded that the person and work of Jesus are intertwined and cannot be neatly separated.

The controversy that led directly to the First Council of Nicaea involved the priest Arius and the bishop of Alexandria named appropriately enough, Alexander. They quarreled over the question, "Is the *Logos* (the Word) from the Gospel of John chapter one, co-eternal with the Father, and thus divine?" Alexander said yes, and Arius said no.

Arius, like most theologians of his day, had been greatly influence by Greek philosophy, particularly Neoplatonism. Neoplatonism perceived perfection as a reality which was impassible (unable to suffer and experience emotion) and immutable (unchangeable). Since God was perfect, that meant God could not change nor could God suffer or experience emotion.[4] If this was true, how could Christians talk about Jesus, a human being who changed from being an infant into an adult, and who was angry and wept, and who suffered on a cross actually be the impassable and immutable God? Moreover, since the world was a place of constant change and suffering, how could the perfect God be directly involved in the world? How could this God even communicate directly with the world?

Arius reasoned that since the Son was passable and mutable, the Son must have been created by God. Thus, the Son was not co-eternal with the Father. Arius and his followers were known to sing a slogan, "There was a time when the Son was not." (We don't know the tune.) No one disputed that the Son existed before the

---

4 I very much disagree with the belief that God is impassable and immutable. If the dictum is true that "if it cannot be said of Jesus, it cannot be said about God" then God reacts emotionally and is affected by change (though God does not change in God's nature).

world. Arius argued that the Son was created before the world. To be created is to place the Son, the *Logos*, in time.

The theologian who would become the champion of the orthodox position was Athanasius. Athanasius argued that since the Word was divine, as John says in his Gospel, "the Word was God" (1:1), and the Word could not be part of creation, the Word could not be created. Judaism had rightly drawn a sharp line between God and creation. Arius, according to Athanasius, had put the Word on the wrong side of the line. Athanasius insisted that the Word was begotten eternally. But what does it mean to be begotten?

WHO'S BEGETTING WHOM? AND WHAT KIND OF BEGETTING IS BEING BEGOTTEN?

The conflict at Nicaea centered around the words "creating" and "begetting" and between "in time" and "eternally." What is the difference between creating and begetting? What does John mean in his Gospel when he says, that "God gave his only begotten Son?" (3:16). Athanasius argued that anything created is made of separate material. A bench has nothing in common with the carpenter. Begotten or "born from" implies that the Son comes out of the Father's substance like a child comes out of her or his parents' substance. Therefore, calling Christ begotten makes him divine and not a creature. Athanasius said that the Father was of the same substance as the Son while Arius argued that the Son was of like substance with the Father.

The debate at Nicaea centered on one little letter in two different Greek words. Was Jesus as Athanasius said of the *same* (*homoousios*) essence with God, or was Arius correct that Jesus was of a *similar* (*homoiousios*) essence. Some have referred to this as "the iota controversy" since the only difference in these two words is the former word has no "i" (in Greek called "iota") while the latter word does. Now, it may seem like a silly debate and somewhat difficult to comprehend the disparity, but there is indeed a difference between what it means to be the same as something and like something. To say that I am the same as Allan Bevere is to say that I am Allan Bevere. But if someone else says, "I am like Allan Bevere," that means while that person is not me, he may share some similarities with me—e.g. facial characteristics, mannerisms. I actually have an identical twin brother, but we are of like substance with each other, not of the same substance. Athanasius' point was that Jesus was *homoousios*; he *was* God. Arius claimed that Jesus was *homoiousios;* he was similar in certain ways, but not actually fully divine.

Athanasius realized that his analogy only went so far.[5] He warned that the begetting of the Son was not exactly like the begetting of a human child. After human children are born, they are dependent upon their parents. The nature of the Son is infinite and eternal, just like the Father. This is where the question of time comes into focus. According to Athanasius there was never a time when the Son was not. If the Son had come into existence in time, then he would have had to undergo change. If the nature of the Son was like ours, being liable to change in his nature, then eventually he might turn to evil ways. How much confidence could Christians have in their salvation if the Savior might change? Notice, once again that the practical question of salvation is raised. In the Old Testament, God's changelessness in reference to his nature is directly related to God's faithfulness to the covenant with Israel.

The First Council of Nicaea sided with Athanasius declaring that Arius' portrait of Jesus failed to accurately complete the Jesus puzzle. Jesus was God. Jesus was *homoousios* with no "i." Jesus was the same essence as God. This meant that Jesus was fully divine, The Council also took great care to reaffirm once again that Jesus was also fully human. This meant that Jesus' divinity did not take away from his humanity and vice versa. Jesus was fully divine and fully human all at the same time. And yet to say that God the Father and God the Son are one God, that is not to say they are not different. Some made an attempt to clarify further in more detail that sameness and difference—what does it mean for Jesus to have

---

5   An analogy is a comparison between two things, but all analogies break down, which means if the comparison is pushed too far, it no longer makes sense. For analogies to make sense, they must be narrowly focused. To say, "The cake was like a rock," is to draw a comparison between the hardness of the cake and the rock. To suggest in that analogy that the cake also tasted like a rock is to take the analogy too far.

a divine and a human nature? The attempted clarifications were not very successful and added to the failed portraits of Jesus.

THE THEANDRIC UNION: WHAT GOD HAS JOINED TOGETHER, LET NO ONE SEPARATE

The question of Christ's divinity was officially settled at Nicaea. However, the debates raged on for centuries afterward. The question of how Christ's divinity and humanity related to each other in the person of Christ still remained.

If we are to understand why these additional portraits of the person of Jesus failed, we must know that the Christian doctrine of the person of Christ focuses on the Theandric Union, of which three questions are asked: 1) Is the Son truly God? 2) Is the Son truly human? 3) If so, how can both affirmations be made together?[6] Jesus was recognized as being human. Such would be obvious to the eye. After his death and resurrection, it became apparent that he was more than human. We know that the earliest affirmation of the church was "Jesus is Lord," a title reserved only for God.

In a monotheistic faith, such as Judaism such a confession caused difficulty. The first Christians, in keeping with their Jewish faith, believed in one God alone. Yet, their experience of Jesus told them that he was more than human. The controversies over the Trinity would elicit an attempt to understand the person of Jesus in his relationship to God the Father, the God of Israel.

Now, on to the failed portraits.

ONE GOD IN TWO NATURES: SOMETIMES LESS IS MORE

In order to understand these additional failed portraits of Jesus we must know that in the fourth century A.D. there were two basic schools of thought in the church, each with a different emphasis— the Antiochene school and the Alexandrian School (named after the cities in which they flourished). Both sides agreed that God was unchangeable and eternal. The disagreement came over the question of how the unchangeable eternal God could be joined to

---

6 Thomas C. Oden, *The Word of Life* (San Francisco: Harper Collins, 1992), p. 164.

a changeable, historical human being. The Alexandrines (like Clement and Origen) emphasized Jesus' divinity. They were concerned that too much emphasis on Jesus' humanity might eclipse his divine nature. The Antiochenes, on the other hand, underscored Jesus' humanity fearing that his divine nature would obscure his clearly human nature. Both sides affirmed Jesus' two natures. At issue was how to understand the relationship between the two.

It is important to note that Antioch and Alexandria were eastern cities of the empire, as was Nicaea. The Christological and trinitarian debates were primarily eastern in origin. In the west, the church had more immediate problems. The barbarian invasions were of such pressing concern that western theologians contented themselves with the formula of the second century bishop, Tertullian—there was one God in three persons or substance. At this moment in history the western church seemed content to leave the solution there. But some eastern theologians were not content with Tertullian's phraseology. They believed more needed to be said about the two natures of Christ.

Apollinaris: Divine Treasure in a Clay Jar

Apollinaris was on the Alexandrian side of the argument. He suggested that the second person of the Trinity, the Word, took the place of the rational soul in Jesus. Basically, Apollinaris was saying hat Jesus had a human body and a divine mind. He asserted that the human mind is subject to great change and prone to fantasize about improper things. Christ's mind was the unchangeable, divine Word. Christ's body was a changeable, developing human body.

This explanation was eventually rejected. The opposition came from the Antiochene school. Jesus must truly be human. This was necessary because Jesus became human that he might save humanity. If Jesus was only partly human then humanity can only partly be saved. If Jesus' mind was not human, then the human mind cannot receive redemption. Gregory of Nazianzus writes,

> For that which he has not taken up he has not saved. He saved that which he joined to his divinity. If only half of Adam had fallen, then it would be possible for Christ to take up and

save only half. But if the entre human nature fell, all of it must be united to the Word in order to be saved as a whole.[7]

Apollinarianism was rejected by the Council of Constantinople in 381 A.D.

THEODORE OF MOPSUESTIA: WILL THE REAL JESUS PLEASE STAND UP?

Apollinarianism was rejected in part due to the arguments of Theodore of Mopsuestia (affectionately known as Teddy the Mop) from the Antiochene School. Teddy suggested that Apollinaris' argument contradicted Scripture. The New Testament describes Jesus as growing in wisdom (Luke 2:52). If Jesus' mind was divine, then Apollinaris would have to conclude that the divine mind was growing in wisdom. Did Apollinaris want to say that?

But Teddy believed it was necessary to do more than put the inadequacies of Apollinaris' position on display. He had to offer an alternative. Teddy stated that Christ had two natures in one person and that he was fully human, not only having a human body. Jesus, Teddy stated, felt pain and had human emotions. But since divinity was not subject to change, Christ's divine nature did not experience human emotions. His position can be explained in this way: the two natures of Christ can be understood as two subjects to which as assigned different predicates—actions that revealed which nature of Christ was doing the acting. When Christ wept or was angry, that was his human nature. When Jesus performed miracles or forgave sins, that was the divine nature.

The problem with Teddy's view is that he gives Jesus two different personalities in one body. Sometimes he acts as God, at other times he acts as human. Not only is such a separation of Jesus' two natures difficult to find in Scripture, it turns Jesus into a bifurcated Savior and when Jesus dies for our salvation, is it the divine or human Jesus? And if it is true that Jesus is Savior precisely because he is divine and human, then it is a huge mistake to assign Jesus' individual actions to one nature or the other. Jesus is Savior because

---

7   Gregory of Nazianzus, *Epistle 101*. See also Gonzalez, *The Story of Christianity*, 1:253.

only God can save. Thus, Jesus must be fully God. Jesus must also be fully human because Jesus cannot save that which he has not become. Jesus is one person with two natures, but those natures do not act independently from each other.

NESTORIUS: THE SCHIZOPHRENIC JESUS

Another theologian who offered an alternative way to understand the person of Christ was Nestorius. Nestorius was from the Antiochene School. Nestorius found himself at the center of controversy when he declared that it was improper to call Jesus' mother, Mary, *theotokos*—the "mother of God," or "God-bearer." Instead, she should be called *christotokos*—the "bearer of Christ." Protestants usually reject the notion of Mary as the *theotokos* because they do not understand what was at stake in this debate that reinforced Mary as the mother of God. When the church affirmed Mary as the *theotokos*, it was not making a divine claim about Mary, it was reinforcing the belief that Jesus was divine. The issue at this point was never about Mary (that would come later); it was about Jesus.

When Nestorius said that Mary was not the God-bearer, he was arguing that distinctions needed to be made between Christ's divinity and humanity. There are some things that can be said about Jesus' humanity that cannot be said about his divinity and vice-versa. Nestorius was attempting to maintain an unqualified belief in the humanity of Jesus and maintain his divinity as well. For Nestorius, calling Mary the bearer of God is like saying that God was two years old when Mary gave birth to Jesus—in other words, how can Mary give birth to God who was already in existence when Jesus was born? If the focus of the title *theotokos* is focused on Mary, then Nestorius' argument seems to make sense, but the focus of the word was never on Jesus' mother.

Like Theodore of Mopsuestia, as with others from the Antiochene School, Nestorius offered a solution that made clear distinctions between Christ's divinity and humanity. They were deeply concerned that if such distinctions were not made, then Jesus' divinity would overwhelm his humanity and Christians would no longer be able to talk of a Savior who was truly human.

Nestorius went even further than Theodore in his assertions about the person of Christ. He stated that not only did Christ have two natures, but two persons as well—one divine and one human. The human nature and person was born to Mary, the divine was not. Nestorius also declared that only Jesus' human person suffered on the cross. The church rightly saw the problem with this—it meant that the salvation of humanity was owed only to a human being and not to God. This was the worst danger in dividing the Savior into two persons. Nestorius had created in effect, a schizoid Jesus.

The chief opponent of Nestorius was Cyril, bishop of Alexandria. Cyril's position was that Christ had two natures in one person. His position sounds much like Theodore's, but it was different in one crucial aspect. Cyril stated that because both natures were united in one person, predicates—actions—belonging to one nature could be applied to the other. The technical term in Latin is *communication idiomatum*, which means the two natures in the one person of Jesus, communicate and act together. Cyril believed that if the one person of Christ could be maintained, his two natures could be spoken of in such a way as to avoid a schizophrenic Jesus.

CONCLUSION: WHEN SILENCE IS GOLDEN

The matter was officially brought to rest at the Council of Chalcedon in 451 A.D. with this official statement:

> Following, then, the holy Fathers, we all with one voice teach that it is to be confessed that our Lord Jesus Christ is one and the same God, perfect in divinity, and perfect in humanity, true God and true human, with a rational soul and a body, of one substance with the Father in his divinity, and of one substance with us in his humanity, in every way like us, with the only exception of sin, begotten of the Father before all time in his divinity, and also begotten in the latter days, in his humanity, of Mary the virgin bearer of God.

This is one and the same Christ, Son, Lord, Only-begotten, manifested in two natures without any confusion, change, division or separation. The union does not destroy the difference of the two natures, but on the contrary the properties of each are kept, and both are joined in on person and *hypostasis* [substance or underlying reality] They are not divided into two persons, but belong to the one Only-begotten Son, the Word of God, the Lord Jesus Christ. All this, as the prophets of old said of him, and as he himself has taught us, and as the Creed of the Fathers has passed on to us.[8]

It is important to note that this statement did not attempt to say more than could be said about Jesus, which was precisely the mode of operation with those who put forth the failed portraits. The statement merely set limits on what could be said about Jesus. It is beyond such limits that error can be found. While Christians must talk about God, it is possible to say too much and find themselves speaking about something that is actually less than God. There are indeed times when less is more. The wisdom of the church councils is reflected in saying what must be said about the God who has come to us in Jesus Christ. In contemplating the divine, there comes a time when silence is the only response. In Jesus Christ, the divine and the human meet. What more needs to be said?

But, our discussion of the Jesus Puzzle would not be complete if we only discussed the failed portraits that have been offered. The church has been blessed that the New Testament offers us different, but complimentary portraits of Jesus that we can trust in order to answer the all-important question, "Who is Jesus?" But first we must have an Interlude on why this entire discussion is important in the first place.

---

8   Quoted in Gonzalez, *The Story of Christianity*, 1:257.

CHAPTER THREE

Interlude: Why Even Bother?

THEOLOGICAL GARDENING: DOCTRINE IS WHAT GROWS FROM THE SEED OF SCRIPTURE

When we look at the four Gospels, even a superficial reading reveals that many of the issues that concerned the church leaders at Nicaea are not present in Matthew, Mark, Luke, or John. There is no mention of *homoousios* (same substance) or *theotokos* (God-bearer) or how to understand the person of Jesus in relationship to his body and soul. To be sure, we do see mention of the *logos* (the Word) and Jesus as begotten in John's Gospel, which were concerns at that first council, but there are plenty of things that cannot *clearly* be found in the four canonical portraits of Jesus. Is it the case, as some suggest, that the early church went off the trail in debating these issues that are not directly mentioned in the Gospels? Would it be better for us simply to forget these theological debates and ignore anything not *explicitly* found in the Bible?

As I respond to these questions, let me offer a brief reminder of two things mentioned earlier: First, the Gospels themselves created a problem that needed to be answered: How is it that Christians can reconcile the affirmation in the Gospels that Jesus is clearly human and yet in some way, divine? This concern was motivated by the very practical question of whether or not Jesus can legitimately be our Savior. Second, the church had to discuss these matters because by the fourth century a huge swath of the church was very divided over this issue and it was fragmenting the church and affecting its mission. Any pastor or leader in the church knows how dangerous it is to ignore big problems in a congregation. Even if there were those who preferred to ignore the problem, the church had no choice but to address it.

So how do the great doctrines of our faith relate to the New Testament when it seems that the New Testament does not specifically and clearly speak of those doctrine? How are our great doctrine legitimately based in Scripture?

I have used the images of the puzzle and the portrait to clarify our subject matter in this book. Now I will employ another image—that of the seed that grows. Jesus himself tells the parable of the mustard seed to illustrate how the Kingdom of God grows in the world (Matthew 13:31-32). It starts as a tiny seed under the soil. As that seed is fed from the soil and refreshed from the rain, it sprouts and grows into a bush large enough for the birds to perch upon it. As a seed, it is almost impossible to imagine what that seed will become. When the fully-grown plant is viewed, it is almost impossible to imagine that it came from a seed smaller than the nail of one's little finger.

With this analogy in mind, think of the Scripture as a field with the seeds already sown underneath the soil. When those seeds are fed and watered by reading and study and prayer and discussion with the desire to understand faith in a fuller way, the plants that spring from the soil of Scripture are the great doctrines of our faith. So, while the doctrine of Jesus' divinity is not present in the Gospels as clearly defined as it was in the Council of Nicaea (and later the Council of Constantinople), it is nevertheless there. And if we can say that the leaders of the church in the fourth century were the gardeners watering the seed of the person of Jesus in the Gospels, the plant that broke through the soil was a more robust account of who Jesus is as God's very presence, and the fruit it ultimately produced are the church's creeds.

But again, it can be asked if this is the best way to read Scripture—developing doctrine not clearly in Scripture? My response is to ask if it is acceptable to interpret Scripture the way Scripture interprets Scripture? Because that is exactly what we have been doing in this book and that's exactly what the church councils did when they met. Let's explore that in more detail.

READING BACKWARD: THE NEW TESTAMENT THROUGH THE LENS OF NICAEA

What if the writers of the Gospels interpreted the Old Testament through the lens of the ministry of Jesus? What if they read backwards from New to Old? Would that justify the backwards reading of the New Testament engaged in by the Council of Nicaea

20

that produced the lens of the creeds through which we see the New Testament today?

There is no doubt that the writers of the Gospels (and the rest of the New Testament) were interpreting the Old Testament through the ministry of Jesus. There is debate as to how to understand their reinterpretation of Israel's Scriptures, but no one doubts they were indeed seeing the Old Testament in light of Jesus.

Richard Hays refers to this practice as reading backwards. He quotes Protestant Reformer, Martin Luther who said that the Old Testament is the "swaddling cloths and the manger in which Christ lies." Hays writes, "Just as Jesus was wrapped in humble swaddling clothes in the manger, so too is he wrapped in the swaddling clothes of the Law, the Prophets, and the Writings."[9]

We saw this earlier with Saul on the Damascus Road. His encounter with the risen Christ made him realize that Jesus was the lens through which to read the Old Testament. In a sense, that is just what we are doing with the creeds the church has given to us. They become the lens by which we understand the New Testament. Just as the Gospel writers viewed the Old Testament through the life, death, and resurrection of Jesus, so the creeds are the product of looking backward to the New Testament's understanding of Jesus and drawing out the fuller implications of his person. The creeds answer in a theological way, "Who is Jesus?"

It is now time to look at the four Gospels and the different, but complimentary portraits of Jesus. It is beyond the scope of this little book to look in detail at each Gospel's portrait since our focus is on Jesus' person as divine and human. What can be done is to sketch a basic outline of each Gospel portrait, focusing on how the Gospels present to us, in their own way, Jesus Christ as the embodiment of the God of Israel.

---

9   Richard Hays, Reading Backwards: *Figural Christology and the Fourfold Gospel Witness* (Waco: Baylor University Press, 2014), p. 1

CHAPTER FOUR

Four Reliable Portraits of Jesus: One Divine Savior

A SAVIOR FOR ALL SEASONS

At the Art Institute of Chicago, a collection of paintings is displayed by impressionist artist, Claude Monet referred to by most simply as "Haystacks." Monet painted a series of twenty-five paintings all depicting the same subject—haystacks in a field against a backdrop of hills. He painted them to demonstrate how they would look at different times of day in different seasons in various kinds of weather. The subject remains the same—haystacks—but they are portrayed differently based on their surroundings

I think that is a good illustration in thinking about Jesus in our four Gospel. Matthew, Mark, Luke, and John are interested mainly in one thing—offering to us a portrait of the same Jesus, but with a particular emphasis that casts light on his life and ministry to highlight a particular aspect of who Jesus is and what Jesus has done. In this way, our four Gospels present to us a Jesus who comes to the world in every and all situations to offer redemption. Each Gospel helps us to understand Jesus in a certain way and when we bring all four Gospel portraits together we see a Savior for all seasons, who is relevant in all times and places.

Let us briefly survey those portraits.

THE GOSPEL WRITERS: THE MONETS OF THE WRITTEN WORD

Each of the four Gospels casts Jesus in a different light to highlight the significance of Jesus. This is understandable since it would be impossible to capture the breadth of the person and work of Jesus in just one written portrait. Jesus was larger than life to his first followers, to those who were present with him throughout his time on earth. Even the four Gospels are unable to say everything that can be said about Jesus—their witness is not exhaustive—but it is sufficient. How does each Gospel point us to Jesus as the divine Savior, the embodiment of the God of Abraham, Isaac, and Jacob?[10]

MARK: HINTS OF THE DIVINE JESUS[11]

In some ways, Mark is a mysterious Gospel dropping hints at who Jesus is but presenting the person of Christ in the context of mystery. Having said that the hint of Jesus' divinity comes to us right at the beginning of Mark:

> The beginning of the good news of Jesus Christ, the Son of God. As it is written in the prophet Isaiah, 'See, I am sending my messenger ahead of you, who will prepare your way; the voice of one crying out in the wilderness: "Prepare the way of the Lord, make his paths straight." (1:1-3)

In verse 4-8, Mark makes it clear that the messenger sent to prepare the way is John the Baptist. The Lord whose way is prepared in Isaiah 40 is clearly the God of Israel. The straight-forward implication here is that Jesus is the Lord, the God of Israel Isaiah expects to come; however, Mark does not come right out and say it. One must read backward and understand Isaiah 40 in its context to see the connection.

There are other passages in Mark where Jesus' divine status is hinted at and can be seen for the discerning reader. In 2:1-12, Jesus heals a paralyzed man after forgiving him of his sins.

---

10 I cannot give an exhaustive account of how each of the four Gospels present us with a divine Jesus. For more detailed treatments see the following: Richard Bauckham, *Jesus and the God of Israel: God Crucified and Other Studies on the New Testament's Christology of Divine Identity.* (Grand Rapids: Eerdmans, 2008); Richard Hays, *Echoes of Scripture in the Gospels* (Waco: Baylor University Press, 2016); Idem., *Reading Backwards*; Larry Hurtado, *One God, One Lord: Early Christian Devotion and Ancient Jewish Monotheism.* (Edinburgh: T&T Clark, 1988); N.T. Wright, *Jesus and the Victory of God.* (Minneapolis: Fortress Press, 1996).

11 The order I am dealing with the four Gospels is chronological, based on the consensus of scholarship. Thus, I begin with Mark, then Matthew, Luke, and finally John.

When Jesus saw their faith, he said to the paralytic, 'Son, your sins are forgiven.' Now some of the scribes were sitting there, questioning in their hearts, 'Why does this fellow speak in this way? It is blasphemy! Who can forgive sins but God alone?' At once Jesus perceived in his spirit that they were discussing these questions among themselves; and he said to them, 'Why do you raise such questions in your hearts? Which is easier, to say to the paralytic, "Your sins are forgiven", or to say, "Stand up and take your mat and walk"? But so that you may know that the Son of Man has authority on earth to forgive sins'—he said to the paralytic— 'I say to you, stand up, take your mat and go to your home.' And he stood up, and immediately took the mat and went out before all of them; so that they were all amazed and glorified God, saying, 'We have never seen anything like this!' (2:5-12)

Notice that nowhere does Mark overtly claim that Jesus is the embodiment of God's presence, but the hint is there in the Pharisees' claim that only God can forgive sin. Moreover, the claim of the people at the end of the story, "We have never seen anything like this," is an invitation to ponder as to why no one has ever witnessed such an amazing event. Perhaps that is because God had never visited his people in embodied form until the person of Jesus.

One last example comes to us from Mark 4—the stilling of the storm. The disciples and Jesus are on the Sea of Galilee when a violent storm appears out of nowhere threatening to sink their small fishing boat. The disciples awaken Jesus in fright and Jesus then acts. "He woke up and rebuked the wind, and said to the sea, 'Peace! Be still!' Then the wind ceased, and there was a dead calm" (4:39). As Mark finishes the story, the disciples' question becomes our question: "'Who then is this, that even the wind and the sea obey him?'" (v. 41). Any hearer of this story familiar with the Old Testament would know the answer that is hinted at in the question. Psalm 107.

Then they cried to the Lord in their trouble,

and he brought them out from their distress;

24

he made the storm be still,

and the waves of the sea were hushed.

Then they were glad because they had quiet,

and he brought them to their desired haven (vv. 28-30).

Nowhere does Mark explicitly identify Jesus with the God of the Hebrew Scriptures, but Mark consistently infers it in his portrait of Jesus. The disciples' question, "Who is this"? is meant to provoke reflection on the possibility that this Jesus may be more than human.[12] In telling the story of Jesus in all of its mystery, Mark offers hints of the divine Jesus that will be discerned only by those "who have ears to hear" (Mark 4:9-12).

MATTHEW: THE EMBODIED PRESENCE OF ISRAEL'S GOD

If Mark's portrait of Jesus hints at his divinity, Matthew' picture is more explicit. In the stilling of the storm in Matthew (8:23-27), the disciples awaken Jesus not by addressing him as teacher as in Mark, but by calling him "Lord." Matthew's Gospel is crafted around the claim in Matthew's birth narrative in chapter 1:

She will bear a son, and you are to name him Jesus, for he will save his people from their sins.' All this took place to fulfil what had been spoken by the Lord through the prophet:

'Look, the virgin shall conceive and bear a son, and they shall name him Emmanuel.' Which means, 'God is with us.' (1:21-23)

It is going too far afield to work through the questions of Matthew's use of Isaiah 7:14, but what is clear is that Matthew 1:23 sets the context for the rest of the Gospel—that Jesus is the

---

12 Larry Hurtado, *Mark: A Good News Commentary* (San Francisco: Harper and Row, 1983), p. 87.

embodiment of the God of Israel and more than Mark presents Jesus as the fulfillment of Israel's story in the Old Testament.

In Matthew, the earthly Jesus is often worshiped—the magi (2:2, 11), a leper, (8:2), an official of the synagogue (9:18), a Canaanite woman (15:25), the mother of James and John (20:20), and worship of the risen Jesus ((28:9), 28:17). It is the case that some of these passages can just as easily be translated as simply bowing to pay respects, but as Hays rightly points out that when understanding these many references in the context of Jesus as "God with Us," it is difficult to conclude that anything less than worship is what is taking place.[13] It must be pointed out that the Greek word for "worship," in Matthew 4:10 (*proskuneó*), which clearly refers to the worship of God, is the same word used in all the other instances just mentioned.

Jesus is also presented as a new Moses who is greater than Moses.[14] In the Sermon on the Mount, Jesus not only quotes and upholds the law, he fulfills it; and Jesus has authority over the law to refract its meaning in a new more intensive light. In chapter five, he states,

> '*You have heard that it was said* to those of ancient times, "You shall not murder"; and "whoever murders shall be liable to judgement." *But I say to you that* if you are angry with a brother or sister, you will be liable to judgement; and if you insult a brother or sister, you will be liable to the council; and if you say, "You fool", you will be liable to the hell of fire (5:21-22)

> '*You have heard that it was said,* "You shall not commit adultery." *But I say to you* that everyone who looks at a woman with lust has already committed adultery with her in his heart. (5:27-28)

> '*It was also said,* "Whoever divorces his wife, let him give her a certificate of divorce." *But I say to you* that

---

13 Hays, *Reading Backward*, pp. 44-45.
14 Scot McKnight, *Sermon on the Mount: The Story of God Commentary* (Grand Rapids: Zondervan, 2013). P. 76.

anyone who divorces his wife, except on the ground of unchastity, causes her to commit adultery; and whoever marries a divorced woman commits adultery (5:31-32)

'Again, *you have heard that it was said* to those of ancient times, "You shall not swear falsely, but carry out the vows you have made to the Lord." *But I say to you,* Do not swear at all, either by heaven, for it is the throne of God, or by the earth, for it is his footstool, or by Jerusalem, for it is the city of the great King (5:33-35).

'*You have heard that it was said,* "An eye for an eye and a tooth for a tooth." *But I say to you,* Do not resist an evildoer. But if anyone strikes you on the right cheek, turn the other also. Matthew 5:38-39

'*You have heard that it was said,* "You shall love your neighbor and hate your enemy." *But I say to you,* Love your enemies and pray for those who persecute you (5:43-44).

In each of these, Jesus reminds his hearers of what the Old Testament Scriptures say in one place or another with the word, "You have heard it said." And then in astonishing fashion, Jesus places himself in authority over the law with the words, "but I say to you." No devout rabbi in Jesus' day would ever dare to be so presumptuous to take such authority reserved only for God who is the lawgiver. (Moses is referred to as the lawgiver, but that actually means he received the law from God.) God gives the law, only God can change or modify it in some way. In Jesus' words the echoes of the divine voice can be heard.

One last passage in Matthew that forces the hearers to draw the conclusion that Jesus is the embodiment of Israel's God is found in Matthew 12:1-8. The disciples are picking heads of grain, gleaning in the fields, on the Sabbath. As often happens the Pharisees are there to accuse Jesus and his followers of breaking the Jewish holy day. In response, Jesus refers to the example of David and his men eating the Bread of Presence in the temple (tabernacle) when they

27

were hungry, something not lawful for them to do. Then Jesus says to the religious leaders, "something greater than the temple is here." In context, Jesus is that something greater. The obvious answer to the question, "What is greater than the temple?" is God; for it is in the temple where God is worshiped.

Finally, in verse 9 we read, "For the Son of Man is lord of the sabbath." Whether Mark is quoting Jesus here or is adding his own commentary, if Jesus, the Son of Man is lord of the sabbath, then he is the giver of the sabbath. No mere human being would claim to be lord of the sabbath for it was God and God alone who instituted the weekly day of rest (Exodus 20:8-11).

Only the one who gives the law, can speak about the law the way Jesus did. Either the Jesus of Matthew is a blasphemer guilty of the worst of all crimes in Judaism, or he is who Matthew claims him to be—The God of Israel come in human flesh.

LUKE: JESUS THE DIVINE SAVIOR

For Luke the entire Old Testament, what he refers to as the Scriptures, bears witness to Jesus as the divine Savior. Luke is not as direct as Matthew in declaring the divinity of Jesus. His connections to the Old Testament are of the nature of "indirect correspondence."[15] In these correspondences, Luke ascribes Old Testament passages to Jesus that in their original context refer to the God of Israel. In the calling of John the Baptist in Luke 3, Luke quotes Isaiah 40 beginning with verse 3:

> The voice of one crying out in the wilderness:
>
> "Prepare the way of the Lord,
>
> make his paths straight.
>
> Every valley shall be filled,
>
> and every mountain and hill shall be made low,
>
> and the crooked shall be made straight,

---

15 Hays, *Reading Backward*, p. 58.

and the rough ways made smooth;

and all flesh shall see the salvation of God" (vv.4-6).

Luke's language in verse 4 should not be missed. "Make *his* [the Lord's] paths straight" in Isaiah's context refers to the God of Israel and Luke applies this to Jesus. The indirect correspondence is almost obvious.

Of the four Gospel writers, Luke most often refers to Jesus as Lord. The Greek word *kurios* is the word employed by the Septuagint to translate the Hebrew *Yahweh*, which is the holiest name for God and used only for the God of Israel throughout the Old Testament.[16] In referring to Jesus as *kurios* so many times, Luke is using these numerous references to build to a crescendo in Acts 10:36, the second volume of Luke's work, where Peter addresses the Roman centurion, Cornelius: "You know the message he sent to the people of Israel, preaching peace by Jesus Christ—he is Lord of all." Jesus, the one who preached the message to God's people is also the Lord of all.[17] It is impossible to conclude that Luke is using *kurios* as nothing more than a title of respect. In Jesus, the God of Israel who is Lord of all is present.

As in Matthew, Jesus is worshiped in Luke's Gospel, though such worship does not take place until the end (24:52), perhaps as part of the crescendo building from the indirect connections to Jesus' Lordship throughout Luke's work. It is intriguing that the only other mention of worship in Luke is found near the beginning during Jesus' temptation where he responds to one of the devil's temptations in quoting Deuteronomy 6:13, "Worship the Lord your God, and serve only him" (Luke 4:8). In Luke, worship is mentioned only twice—the first reference affirming the worship of the God of Israel alone, and the second with the disciples worshiping Jesus.

Another reference that corresponds Jesus to the God of Israel comes from the mouth of Jesus himself,

---

16 See C. Kavin Rowe, *Early Narrative Christology: The Lord in the Gospel of Luke* (Grand Rapids: Baker Academic, 2009).
17 Hays, *Reading Backward*, p. 64.

"Jerusalem, Jerusalem, the city that kills the prophets and stones those who are sent to it! How often have I desired to gather your children together as a hen gathers her brood under her wings, and you were not willing! See, your house is left to you. And I tell you, you will not see me until the time comes when you say, 'Blessed is the one who comes in the name of the Lord.'" (13:34-35).

The Old Testament depicts God as the one who protects Israel utilizing the imagery of a mother bird protecting her brood under her wings (Deuteronomy 32:1-12 and Psalm 91:1-4). What is significant is that Jesus does not refers to God as the one who desires to gather his people for safety, but he refers to himself. Moreover, he states, "how often have I desired." This cannot refer only to the few short months that the earthly Jesus was in Jerusalem, seemingly in Luke his one and only visit. This is a reference to the repeated rejection of God by God's people throughout Israel's history.

One final example comes from the well-known post-resurrection story of the Emmaus Road in Luke 24.

Now on that same day two of them were going to a village called Emmaus, about seven miles from Jerusalem, and talking with each other about all these things that had happened. While they were talking and discussing, Jesus himself came near and went with them, but their eyes were kept from recognizing him. And he said to them, 'What are you discussing with each other while you walk along?' They stood still, looking sad. Then one of them, whose name was Cleopas, answered him, 'Are you the only stranger in Jerusalem who does not know the things that have taken place there in these days?' He asked them, 'What things?' They replied, 'The things about Jesus of Nazareth, who was a prophet mighty in deed and word before God and all the people, and how our chief priests and leaders handed him over to be condemned to death and crucified him. But we had hoped that he was the one to redeem Israel (vv. 13-21)

Here the hope of the two on the road to Emmaus was that Jesus was *the* redeemer of Israel, not the one through whom God would save, but the Savior himself. It is abundantly clear from the Old Testament that it is Israel's God who is the redeemer.

Do not fear, you worm Jacob,
you insect Israel!
I will help you, says the Lord;
your Redeemer is the Holy One of Israel
(Isaiah 41:14)

We cannot help but be reminded of Athanasius' argument that Jesus can only be referred to as Savior if he is divine because only God can save. For Luke, the God of Israel who redeems Israel and offers that redemption to the entire world is none other than Jesus Christ.

JOHN: THE HUMAN JESUS IS THE DIVINE WORD

Whereas Matthew, Mark, and Luke are more or less subtle concerning the divinity of Jesus, John is very clear—Jesus is the very glory of God in human flesh, the divine Word that speaks creation into existence. It was the conclusion of much biblical scholarship of the nineteenth and twentieth centuries that John's high Christology pointed to a late date for John's Gospel—at least one hundred years after the ministry of Jesus—which was necessary for the development of the human Jesus into the divine Christ. Thankfully, more mainstream scholarship today has rightly argued that the such a high estimation of the divine Jesus occurred much earlier in the first Christian communities.[18]

The opening chapter of John leaves little doubt as to the claim of who Jesus is. He is the Word from the beginning through whom all things were created (1:1-4). The ancient rabbis had much to say about the significance of word and wisdom. Some suggested that both were housed within the Temple and revealed the presence of God.[19] This Word became flesh in Jesus Christ and as John testi-

---

18 See Larry Hurtado, *How on Earth Did Jesus Become a God? Historical Questions about Earliest Devotion to Jesus.* (Grand Rapids: Eerdmans, 2005).

19 Tom Wright, *John for Everyone, Part One* (Louisville: W/JKP, 2004), p. 4.

fies, "has dwelt among us... we have seen his glory" (1:14). The Greek word translated "dwelt" is *eskēnōsen*, whose pronunciation is a reminder of the Hebrew word *shekinah*, refers to the revelation of the very glory of God at the Red Sea, the Mount Sinai, and in the Tabernacle, the portable Temple that traveled with God's people during the wilderness wanderings (Exodus 33:7-11 and 40:34-38). Jesus is the walking Temple of God revealing God's glory wherever he travels.

John also presents the divine character of Jesus in seven "I am" sayings:

> "I am the bread of life; he who comes to me shall not hunger" (6:35).

> "I am the light of the world; he who fallows Me shall not walk in the darkness, but shall have the light of life" (8:12).

> "I am the gate; if anyone enters through Me, he shall be saved, and shall go in and out, and find pasture" (10:9).

> "I am the good shepherd; the good shepherd lays down His life for His sheep." (10:11)

> "I am the resurrection and the life; he who believes in Me shall live even if he dies" (11:25).

> "I am the way, and the truth, and the life; no one comes to the Father, but through Me" (14:6).

> "I am the true vine, and My Father is the vinedresser." (15:1).

These sayings are meant to elicit Moses' discussion with God on Mount Sinai where Moses asks God his name. "God said to Moses, 'I am who I am'" (Exodus 3:15). Here we have the revelation of the sacred name of God, *Yahweh*. In John, Jesus is claiming that he is the One who revealed himself to Moses on the mountain where Moses received the law.

If there is any doubt that John is making such a connection, chapter eight leaves no room for skepticism.

> Jesus said to them, 'Very truly, I tell you, before Abraham was, I am.' So, they picked up stones to throw at him, but Jesus hid himself and went out of the temple (8:58).

Jesus clearly states his existence before the life of the patriarch, Abraham. Moreover, employing the term "I am" makes it obvious that he is not a created being before creation—remember Arius?—but the God of Israel, the preexistent One through whom all things were created.

Just two chapters later the crescendo builds with a direct claim of divinity from Jesus.

> "The Father and I are one." The Jews took up stones again to stone him. Jesus replied, "I have shown you many good works from the Father. For which of these are you going to stone me?" The Jews answered, "It is not for a good work that we are going to stone you, but for blasphemy, because you, though only a human being, are making yourself God" (10:30-34).

In both cases, we see the religious leaders attempting to stone Jesus for blasphemy. First century Jews were strictly monotheistic and staunchly refused to portray Israel's God with any earthly image. Jesus is claiming to reflect in a decisive way God's image in the world. For the Pharisees, Jesus' claims were as pagan as Caesar's claims to divinity. But for John there was nothing non-Jewish about Jesus. In fact, as the other three Gospels attest, Moses and the prophets testified to Jesus.

The four canonical Gospels present four portraits of Jesus. Those portraits are diverse with different emphases, but in all their diversity they also present a complimentary picture. Each Gospel makes its own case both subtly and directly—Jesus is the God of Israel. Such a claim ultimately defies understanding, but it also makes sense. When we read backward from the life of Jesus, Israel's Scriptures come into focus.

Conclusion

Reading Backward, Moving Forward

Context is everything in understanding. Without it, the present moment is subject to interpretive whims of our own making. The New Testament writers experienced the ministry of Jesus and because of his resurrection were forced to make sense of it all by going to the only place possible—their Scriptures—the Old Testament. In the same way, the second and third generations of Christians too had to make sense of the questions that inevitably arose in the Gospel proclamation. How is it that Jesus can be Savior? What does it mean when the New Testament affirms Jesus' Lordship? What does Jesus' work on our behalf mean for who Jesus is?

In order to answer these questions more fully, the church fathers and mothers did exactly what the writers of the New Testament did—they read backward into the New Testament to bring the picture of Jesus into more detailed focus. And while the church does not claim that the theologizing of Irenaeus, Athanasius, and Augustine among others is Scripture, their work has given to us an authoritative account of the plant that grows and blooms from the seed of Scripture—Christology. Just as a gardener can recognize what plants grow from which seed, so those theological gardeners have identified in their intellectual labors the Tree of Life that brings salvation. That Tree is, as the Nicene Creed affirms, is Jesus Christ, Light of Light, very God of very God. And that God has come to us with a human face, for us and for our salvation.

The gift we have received in our forebears reading backward, makes it possible for us to move forward as God's people who have recognized the time of our visitation by God in Jesus Christ. Our mission remains the same as the instruction given to the women at the empty tomb two thousand years ago—"Go and tell" (Mark 16:7).

Those who have gone before us have given us the content of the message. We don't get to make it up to suit us or the current age. We just get to proclaim it.

Thanks be to God!

TOPICAL LINE DRIVES

Straight to the Point in under 44 Pages

All Topical Line Drives volumes are priced at $5.99 print and $2.99 in all ebook formats.

Available

The Authorship of Hebrews: The Case for Paul	David Alan Black
What Protestants Need to Know about Roman Catholics	Robert LaRochelle
What Roman Catholics Need to Know about Protestants	Robert LaRochelle
Forgiveness: Finding Freedom from Your Past	Harvey Brown, Jr.
Process Theology: Embracing Adventure with God	Bruce Epperly
Holistic Spirituality: Life Transforming Wisdom from the Letter of James	Bruce Epperly
To Date or Not to Date: What the Bible Says about Pre-Marital Relationships	D. Kevin Brown
The Eucharist: Encounters with Jesus at the Table	Robert D. Cornwall
The Authority of Scripture in a Postmodern Age: Some Help from Karl Barth	Robert D. Cornwall
Rendering unto Caesar	Chris Surber
The Caregiver's Beattitudes	Robert Martin
What is Wrong with Social Justice	Elgin Hushbeck, Jr.
I'm Right and You're Wrong	Steve Kindle
Words of Woe: Alternative Lectionary Texts	Robert D. Cornwall
Stewardship: God's Way of Recreating the World	Steve Kindle
Those Footnotes in Your New Testament	Thomas W. Hudgins
Jonah: When God Changes	Bruce G. Epperly
Ruth & Esther: Women of Agency and Adventure	Bruce G. Epperly
Constructing Your Testimony	Doris Horton Murdoch
A Short Critique of Climate Change	Elgin Hushbeck, Jr.
Christianity: The Basics	Elgin Hushbeck, Jr.
The Energy of Love: Reiki and Christian Healing	Bruce Epperly
Process Spirituality	Bruce Epperly
To Be or Not to Be	David Moffett-Moore
Process and Ministry	Bruce Epperly
Process Theology and Celtic Wisdom	Bruce Epperly
One World: The Lord's Prayer from a Process Perspective	Bruce Epperly
A Holy Mystery: Taking Apart the Trinity	Chris Eyre
Process and Pastoral Care	Bruce Epperly
Doing Apologetics	Elgin Hushbeck, Jr.

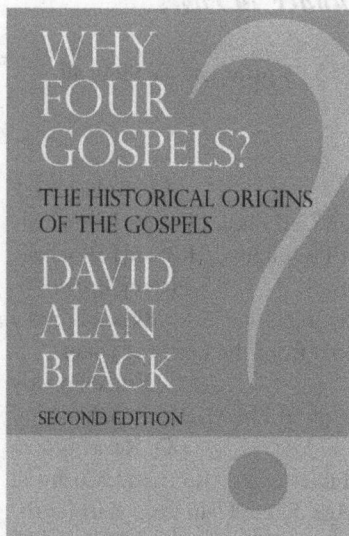

WHY
FOUR
GOSPELS?
THE HISTORICAL ORIGINS
OF THE GOSPELS

DAVID
ALAN
BLACK

SECOND EDITION

Black has given us a refreshing reac-
quisition of the voice of the patristic
fathers in the attempt to discover
the origins of the four Gospels.

Michael J. Wilkins
Professor of New Testament
Language and Literature
Talbot School of Theology,
Biola University

ALSO BY ALLAN R. BEVERE

CRITICAL CHRISTIAN ISSUES VOLUME III
Allan R. Bevere and David Alan Black, General Editors

The Politics
of Witness
The Character of the Church in the World

Allan R. Bevere

Allan Bevere, an ecclesial theologian,
combines in this book a wonderful
"church as politics" with gospel in a
wise, warm, and challenging manner.

Scot McKnight
Julius R. Mantey Professor
of New Testament
Northern Seminary, Lisle, IL.

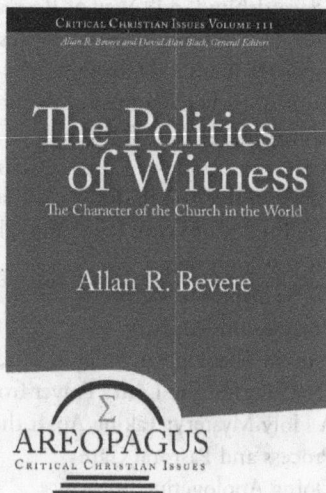

Σ
AREOPAGUS
CRITICAL CHRISTIAN ISSUES

* 9 7 8 1 6 3 1 9 9 6 9 3 1 *